Will you Be Home for Dinner?

Will you Be Home for Dinner?

Recipe Book and topics for raising healthy kids

Tany Thomas

XULON PRESS

Xulon Press
2301 Lucien Way #415
Maitland, FL 32751
407.339.4217
www.xulonpress.com

© 2019 by Tany Thomas

All rights reserved solely by the author. The author guarantees all contents are original and do not infringe upon the legal rights of any other person or work. No part of this book may be reproduced in any form without the permission of the author. The views expressed in this book are not necessarily those of the publisher.

Unless otherwise indicated, Scripture quotations taken from the King James Version (KJV) – *public domain.*

Printed in the United States of America.

ISBN-13: 978-1-54566-382-0

Table of Contents

John 6:35

Then Jesus declared, "I am the bread of life. Whoever comes to me will never go hungry, and whoever believes in me will never be thirsty."

Why this Book vii
Dedication xi
Acknowledgements xiii

Chapter 1: Meal Management 1
Chapter 2: Breakfast at Tiffany's 17
Chapter 3: Setting the Table 31
Chapter 4: Lunch 37
Chapter 5: The School of Manners 51
Chapter 6: Dinner & Conversation 63
Chapter 7: The Clean Up 83
Chapter 8: Desserts! 87

Post Script 103
About the Author 105

Introduction

Why this Book

Genesis 1:29

Then God said, "I give you every seed-bearing plant on the face of the whole earth and every tree that has fruit with seed in it. They will be yours for food."

The scriptures at the beginning of each chapter will be a light for your path to gather your family, nurture life through food and build healthy families.

I've searched high and low for the answers to why I'm here, what is my legacy, and what will I be known and remembered for. Despite all the training, schooling, work experience, and many jobs the one thing that I've done totally lead by instincts and God has been my parenting. I've raised my children and served as a mother figure to others out of pure dedication to their success, growth, and happiness. Parental love is a truly pure desire that knows no boundaries or limitations. If a child needs it then I am going to try to provide. In doing so, I realized that has been my true one and only calling, to be there for others and perhaps even inspire. It is one that provides me with direction and inspiration for most of my life.

As I have considered the specific successes of my life's calling, it brings me to the table where I sat and shared each moment of my children's growth. It was the place for tears, correction, and celebration. I recognized that the primary place where all of our family memories occurred was at the family table. So much of what we plan to do or telling of what we have done is shared at the table among families, so it is at that place where I want to tell parents, this is where they should devote some time planning for the life that will be shared in that spot. No longer is it just a piece of wood and nails propping up the centerpiece or a candle, the lingering place for mail that just won't go away, or the despicable place for crumbs from the dinner last night. It is the focal point and command central of the lively and active family. It is the place where you go to pray, study, nourish, and revive, perhaps take a moment to reflect, share a secret with a friend, or where even your mom sits and watches her legacy. It is the place where the foundation of the home is confirmed through paying bills, it is the place where each year's candles will celebrate another year of life for each member of the family. It is the life blood of the family and for that we need to acknowledge and celebrate its existence! Yes, we need to acknowledge that it exists and its role in keeping the family focused and moving forward.

This book is about creating a valuable formula for sharing and caring for those you love and focusing on how we can further enhance our families by paying attention to what is happening at the table. So, this book is about creating a valuable formula for sharing and caring for those you love and focusing on how we can further enhance our families by paying attention to what is happening at the table. Of course, the other thing that is happening at the table….eating!!! Keep in mind, being a healthy family doesn't just entail eating healthy foods. Kids these days are heavily impacted by the bombarding social pressures that surround them. Establishing routines and focused family time helps to filter out the external influences, which helps mold a well rounded individual.

So, this book shares helpful tips for parenting, organizing the kitchen and recipes that are nutritious as well as easy and fast to prepare. The simple recipes are designed to give you a strong base for your cooking repertoire from which you will build. Use

Why this Book

this book to capture ideas for meals and cooking. It can be your "kitchen bible" where you get inspiration and keep notes of how to structure ideal family time! Because, once the meal is done, family time can begin! My goal for this book is to encourage families whether they be single mothers or fathers or include mother and father, or even extended or unique variations of "parental units." This book can be used by anyone who wants to be the master of their kitchen, anyone who wants to be better at communicating with their family, and anyone who wants to have a more deliberate way of creating their meals. You can use this book if you are a vegan, or if you eat meat. Don't forget to engage the entire family in the healthy and quick meals to help get the food to the table and to foster togetherness. I hope you will take the hints and suggestions to higher levels and that you and your family will be closer and healthier after incorporating healthy family rituals at your table. You can find other helpful tips, tools, and ideas on my website www.pamperedchef.biz/tanyskitchen.

Dedication

To all the single parents doing the most and leaving it all the table each day for their kids.

Acknowledgements

To my beautiful babies that are the inspiration for my life,
and have made my life as a Mom a joy. Their unconditional love and support
helped in the development of this book. Thank you for always believing in me.

Chapter 1

Meal Management

Genesis 6:21

As for you, take for yourself some of all food which is edible, and gather it to yourself, and it shall be for food for you and for them."

Of all the things that we do to provide a loving home for our kids, perhaps the most important thing we can do is sit down with them to have a meal. After all, eating together is an American and world-wide pastime. People all over the world know and understand that sharing a meal with someone can be very intimate and can create a strong bond among those who share an eating experience.

Why then do we not make this a priority for our families? Frequently we become too busy to plan, shop, organize, and cook? I know from experience that it is next to impossible when one child has to be at ballet at 6:00 p.m. and the other has to be at basketball at 6:30, and you work to be able to put something on the table within a measly hour before the start of the evening activities. That is where strategic meal planning and total household organization comes into play.

Once when I visited Hong Kong, our hosts graciously served a wonderful meal promptly at 5pm. I marveled at the usefulness of having a personal chef and how like magic food appeared. Our host for the visit would calmly mention to Meli what she wanted to serve for dinner, and how it should be prepared, and off she would go to a tennis lesson, and off Meli would go to the market to create the perfect meal. If only we had a Meli to organize our meals. During that visit, I came to realize there is a whole profession around domestic management and all the things that go into providing meals for a family and maintaining the kitchen. I've known people to say that the kitchen is the "Women's Office". Well that does sound chauvenistic but someone has to do it. So, it can be a deliberate assignment, shared, or contracted out, but a real focused look at how the kitchen works and is a central part of the family is needed! Go ahead, own it.

Getting organized in the kitchen to be able to provide a nutritious meal for your family on the go is not that hard if you take a few positive steps towards effective planning. I believe there are essentially ten tips to an effectively run Meal Management Program. I call it "MMP". Here are the core guidelines:

1) Always use the bulk purchasing power of a major food outlet like Sam's Club and BJ's Wholesale Club.
2) Prepare larger meals on the weekends; Saturday and Sunday are big cooking days.
3) Prepare two meats on Saturday.
4) Package leftover starches in storage bags for meals later in the week.
5) Keep a well-stocked pantry with certain key staples so that easy meals can be developed.
6) Design a kitchen cleaning schedule that includes kids and other family members.
7) Weekly menu planning.
8) Shopping with a list ensures ability to be ingredient ready! And of course:
9) Ensure your "freezer game" works.
10) Consider planning meals for a month.

I can't speak enough about how useful it is to spend a portion of your food dollars at a bulk buying warehouse. This became easier for me as my children got older, and I had a larger income to invest. Because truly that is the issue. When I first started going to these places, I thought *I never leave here without spending over $100.00, and I don't seem to have anything*. Well at that time, I didn't have a good understanding of what bulk buying could do and what it couldn't do. First of all, it can save you lots of time and money, on daily meal staples for example, purchasing a case of instant oatmeal, lunch meat, or breakfast sausage can give you the quantities you need at a lower price than if you simply went to the grocery store, where you would get less and pay more. After I started buying in bulk, I realized that I had more time, and went to the grocery store less. I also didn't run out of food as quickly.

Starting this system is costly at first, as you invest in your future meals now. Also, there is a need to develop a food storage system that includes managing pantry space and storage containers. With the correct instruments for "MMP", you will be able to breeze through meal planning and save cooked meals for later use in the week or the next week. An important thing to remember is that, you will have to go to the grocery store for perishable items, like bread, milk, and fresh fruits and vegetables (although they can also be purchased in bulk if you have the appropriate space for storing). It may seem like this is a lot of thought and time in planning this part of your life, but if you do not invest the time, you are wasting time, money, and not having the opportunity to sit with your kids where all the fun begins to happen (I'll explain later).

Another trick that should be part of the initial investment is a trip to the store for staples and the creation of the ever important pantry. I am speaking of seasonings, tomato sauce, and other cooking ingredients. I have included a list of staple pantry items that will help make the most of your meal planning. There is nothing worse than realizing you are out of an ingredient and must stop cooking to go out and get it. That used to happen to me so much that some of my friends suggested I make a list when I shop, but I always insisted that I can remember what is needed. Of course, I do buy the occasional second bottle of ketchup not remembering that one is already open in the refrigerator. The reason I stand by this bulk purchasing recommendation is that I hate to grocery shop and wish I had learned how to create this system earlier, so all of you moms and dads out there get this system down and create more time for your family and enjoy each other at mealtime.

Every Sunday should be "sit down and eat together day" around the country. I instituted this rule when my kids were in their early years of high school. I realized that we were each grabbing food and disappearing into the house or worse yet, not having anything substantial. The breakdown of our family eating at that point can be directly attributed to me being a single mother, not having an appropriate in-house support system, and my son getting involved in athletics at a pretty high level. He was traveling all over the region and guess who was going with him; me. So, there was no time to plan meals, much less time to get little ingredients from the store. It was simply grab and go. When I saw him eating like an animal from spending too much time with the coaches and other boys, I knew it was time to focus on my home training. You know we say that all the time, "He/She has no home training." Guess who is responsible for that? You. So, sitting down and eating and talking starts at where? Home. I know many of my friends and family had also fallen victim to activity overload. I am happy I invested my time in that way, because I feel that my kids can sit at a meal with others and not embarrass themselves (or me). After my children became teens and were able to drive, I had a bit of my time back, and I was better able to manage the meal planning; and I proposed a moratorium on Sunday activities and that dinner would be a family affair. We could invite people over, but we would have a family dinner every Sunday. This became a highly valued part of our family time. It was not just the dinner we ate, but the laughs we had, and the time to reflect on the past week and discuss our plans for the upcoming week.

That brings me to weekend cooking; it is important that you cook large portions of whatever you make. I would do a large pan of chicken and freeze some for the next week and use some for one to two meals in the current week. Several variations included barbeque chicken where I would cover the meat in sauce, another day would be chicken salad where I would cut up the breast on salad. So, the trick here is to make enough for meals in the week and for the next week. You only have to get through four days, because everyone knows that Friday is the cook's day off!

There are many variations for getting the meals together by cooking in advance and storing or hosting a Sunday potluck that rotates among family or neighbors. In my case, my friends and I would get together and select dishes to bring to the feast. Of course, all would prepare side dishes in large quantities to share. This is a very successful way of co-op, and one that will bring you closer to your friends and teach the kids a sense of community. I encourage you to try to establish a Sunday co-op meal sharing opportunity.

Another effective way to get ahead of the game during the busy week is to prepare two meals on Saturday. Again, this is predicated on the notion that you have ingredients ahead of time if you can manage Thursday night shopping, then you have what you need.

Saturday can be for meatloaf, one pot chili, and spaghetti. Sunday for chicken, pork, or beef casseroles. Cooking larger portions and great storage is critical to saving time during the week.

Management Cycle

Sunday: Sunday dinner (prepare a large amount of meat (casserole)/starch)
Monday: Never cook—Leftover day 1 (Saturday meal)
Tuesday: Prepare meal from easy prepare options

Wednesday: Eat chicken/beef/pork—Leftover day 2 (Sunday meal)
Thursday: Prepare meal from easy preparation options. Shopping
Friday: Eat out or pizza night!
Saturday: Prepare One Pot Meals/Chicken or Fish

There are of course many barriers to cooking and preparing meals. Overall to be a good cook you must do exactly that….COOK! Practice makes perfect. You have to prepare to cook, so that means giving some thought to the types of things you want to eat during the week, that way when you grocery shop, you can get all the little obscure ingredients you need. The biggest frustration is not having the right ingredient on hand, so think ahead and pick it up.

Other tactics to overcome cooking barriers is to think way ahead and get food out of the freezer in the morning; chop and store some items that are used frequently in dishes; and to get the best flavor ever, you may need to season over night. So that takes planning, but remember this is all for the bigger goal of being ready to bring your family to the table to enjoy the love!!!

The last big tip on being prepared to cook is, pick several dishes everyone loves and stock up on ingredients and make it over and over for a while until it becomes automatic. (Every good cook has their go to meals.) It is at this time that you will be able to add the recipe to your repertoire. In time you will know without thinking what you need to put into the dish; when you get to that level, you will even be able to smell when it is done. In cooking you use all your senses; Seeing if what you are cooking is the right size or color, does it smell right? How does it feel? even listening for those alarms. Go ahead, do a taste test while your cooking and give yourself a chance to gain that experience with your creations. Trust me, it will make you an awesome Chef for your family.

Pantry Shopping List

Olive oil

Vegetable oil

Seasonings (garlic salt, garlic powder, onion salt & powder, chipotle, red pepper flakes, rosemary, dried chives, parsley, Italian seasoning, salt, pepper, cinnamon, nutmeg, paprika)

Pasta (Penne, Spaghetti, Fusilli, Tagliatelle, maccaroni).

Rice (Risotto, Brown, Basmati)

All-purpose flour

Sugar

Beans (variety)

Canned diced tomatoes (variety)

Nuts

Canned meats (fish, tuna, salmon, marcel)

Canned fruit & pie filling (Peaches, apples, cherry)

Pancake mix

Oatmeal

Artichoke

Sun dried tomatoes

Olives

Variety of soups (tomato, cream of mushroom, cream of shrimp etc.)

Chocolate/yellow/white cake mix

Brownie mix

Chocolate chips

Mayo

Salad dressing

Ketchup

BBQ Sauce

Peanut butter

Will you Be Home for Dinner?

Jelly
Shortening
Chicken stock (bouillon cubes)
Pasta sauce, Marinara sauce
Cereal
Tomato sauce
Quick bread mix
Bread crumbs
Vanilla extracts (almond, lemon)
Baking soda, powder
Canned milk, evaporated, sweetened
Simmer Sauces (Thai, Indian)
Baked beans

My Pantry Shopping List

Will you Be Home for Dinner?

My Recipe Ideas

Ingredients

Directions

My Recipe Ideas

Ingredients

_____ _____

_____ _____

_____ _____

_____ _____

_____ _____

_____ _____

_____ _____

Directions

_____

_____

_____

_____

_____

_____

_____

_____

_____

Will you Be Home for Dinner?

My Recipe Ideas

Ingredients

Directions

Meal Management

My Recipe Ideas

Ingredients

Directions

Will you Be Home for Dinner?

My Recipe Ideas

Ingredients

Directions

NOTES

Chapter 2

Breakfast at Tiffany's

Proverbs 31:15

She rises while it is still night and gives food to her household and portions to her maidens.

Breakfast must be the easiest meal of the day, since to "break the fast" you can go as easy as a handful of nuts and juice or brunch! I like a high energy start to the day but small, and a larger lunch, but for kids it may be the opposite!

I never let my children go to school hungry. I had prepared their breakfast when they were younger and supervised and facilitated them eating breakfast when they were older. I always find it hard to understand when a child or teen is over, and you ask them if they are hungry at breakfast time and they say no. No? I'm thinking, "You need to fuel your growing brain, provide for your energy needs and get the protein you need for your growing bones." This also helps kids be awake and lively in their early classes and helps them not to be so hungry at noon that you over do it on sugary snacks and other non- nutritious foods. So, don't go for the I'm too late to eat or other excuses. Kids need a good breakfast.

Note: So important to start the family off on their day with breakfast. This can be a useful time to make sure they are ready for the day, instill personal responsibility (they help prepare and clean up after) and reinforce expectations for behavior and civility. Also, using that morning gathering to send the kids out the door with love and encouragement will always be a happy memory for me and surprisingly for them too. Granted they may be sleep walking at that time, but that time is buried deep in their memories!

Keeping with modern clean eating approaches, I'm moving away from animal meats and doing less bacon and sausage, but weekends, holidays, and guests… it's a go!

When I could, I provided homemade oatmeal. It's so easy to make, and each bowl costs a few cents. With toast and tea and sliced oranges…yummy! Substitute the oatmeal for a cold cereal with wheat and raisins. At times, a boiled egg and strips of bacon, after holiday ham. Always keep a disposable bowels and containers available to send out the door with a rushing teen, they will thank you later.

There are lots of easy breakfasts to streamline the preparation of a healthy meal, and the power you will be giving to your child's brain will go a long way towards improved concentration in the classroom. Here are a couple of easy ideas for breakfast.

BREAKFAST

Fried Southwest Potatoes

Ingredients

4 large Idaho potatoes (4 cups)
1 medium onion
¼ cup vegetable oil
½ tsp. salt
½ tsp. pepper
½ tsp. garlic powder
½ tsp. chipotle seasoning
½ tsp red pepper

Directions

Fill a medium bowl with cold water.
Combine all seasoning in small cup.
Peel potatoes, dice, add to cold water.
Remove outer layer of onion and dice.
Use heavy skillet heat ½ of the oil.
Add onions cook until slightly wilted and turning brown
Using a handful of potatoes at a time place in skillet enough to fill bottom of pan. Sprinkle with seasoning. Allow to brown using spatula to turn after 5 minutes on all sides to ensure the potatoes do not stick. Cook for 15 minutes

Turn heat down and cover for 5 minutes. Flip potatoes and cook another 5 minutes covered. Repeat with other half of oil and remainder of potatoes.

Tip: You can cover and refrigerate diced potatoes in water for 2-3 days, so chop up As many potatoes as you want (keep covered in water)! Store any unused onions in a zip lock in freezer.

Will you Be Home for Dinner?

Spinach, Egg, and Toast

Ingredients
4 eggs
1 tbsp. butter
Salt & pepper to taste
3 tbsp. grated cheese
1/3 cup fresh spinach
Raisin toast

Variation: Salsa and wheat toast

Directions
In medium bowl, beat eggs.
Melt butter in skillet pour eggs, sprinkle top with chopped spinach and cook for 2 minutes then scramble; Salt and pepper.
Add cheese to top of egg to melt.
Turn off stove.
Cover, turn down temp & cover
Make toast, butter top.
Cut spinach egg into 4 pieces top toast.
Serve with fruit.

Green Smoothie

Ingredients
2 frozen ripe bananas

Handful spinach

Handful frozen fresh strawberries

Glass of cold water

(can add frozen blueberries)

Directions
In the blender add in this order: spinach, bananas, strawberries, water. Blend on high until smooth

French Toast Casserole

Ingredients

1 large loaf sourdough or French bread (10 cups)

½ cup chopped pecans

5 large eggs

1 ½ c whole milk

¼ c granulated sugar

Zest medium orange

½ tsp. ground cinnamon

¼ tsp. salt

Directions

Preheat oven 375 degrees F.

Slice bread into 1-inch cubes.

Layer bread and pecans in baking greased dish (2 quart-thick, 3 quart-thin).

Wisk eggs, milk, sugar, orange zest, cinnamon. Pour over bread.

Melt butter, add sugar, and cinnamon spoon drizzle over top.

Bake 35-45 minutes.

Dust with powdered sugar.

Blueberry Muffins

Ingredients

1 cup rinsed blueberries

2 cups all-purpose flour

½ cup granulated sugar

3 tsp. baking powder

½ tsp. salt

1 egg slightly beaten

1 tsp. finely grated orange peel

¼ cup unsalted butter (melted and cooled)

1 cup milk or ½ cup milk and ½ cup buttermilk

Directions

Prepare pan with cupcake liners.

Preheat oven to 375 degrees F.

Toss blueberries with ¼ cup flower in a bowl, set aside.

Sift the remaining flour with the sugar, baking powder, and salt in large bowl.

Stir in egg, orange peel, butter, and milk.

Gentilly fold in blueberries.

Spoon batter into greased 12-muffin pan filling each cup 2/3 full.

Bake 20-25 minutes until golden brown.

Remove from oven and allow to stand 5 minutes before removing from cupcake liner.

Will you Be Home for Dinner?

My Recipe Ideas

Ingredients

Directions

My Recipe Ideas

Ingredients

Directions

Will you Be Home for Dinner?

My Recipe Ideas

Ingredients

Directions

My Recipe Ideas

Ingredients

_____   _____

_____   _____

_____   _____

_____   _____

_____   _____

_____   _____

_____   _____

Directions

_____

_____

_____

_____

_____

_____

_____

_____

Will you Be Home for Dinner?

My Recipe Ideas

Ingredients

Directions

NOTES

Chapter 3

Setting the Table

Psalm 23:5

You prepare a table before me in the presence of my enemies, you have anointed my head with oil, my cup overflows.

Genesis 18:8

So, Abraham hurried into the tent to Sarah, and said, "Quickly, prepare three measures of fine flour, knead it and make bread cakes."

There are three primary table settings at my home: weekdays, Sundays, and holidays. You always know you are welcome to dinner by the way the table is set for eating. Is your table full of crumbs from the meal prior, are the placemats dingy, soiled, and in need of replacement, or do you have letters and mail filling up your table? Believe me I know what a kitchen table attracts. It is like a magnet for everything that must be done right now. Things you don't want to forget as you leave the house, your handbag or mail of an urgent nature. It can run the gamut and rightly so. If that does not illustrate that the table is the focal point for the family, I don't know what else does.

Even more reason for you to take time to really make sure that the primary, sole purpose of the table is to break bread and hold sacred family communications. That is the reason I work hard to find places for those pesky items that the table attracts. I like my table to say, "Hello please sit down, there will be something coming shortly for you to enjoy!" Fresh, colorful linen is a must, and seasonal changes are just as important. An easy one is Christmas since it is easy for me to get my varied green, red, and plaid table cloths out and place my Christmas plates close at hand. I love to have a fitting centerpiece in the middle for when we are not sitting at the table to be a decorative delight to the room.

Flowers also help to make the table special. Ideally the flowers would be brought to the home by a loving partner, but that's just my romantic side talking. Anyone can bring the flowers, (mostly me). I remember very clearly my children picking the neighbors' flowers or the community landscape flowers to bring home to Mama. Of course, after telling them not to do that again, they made a beautiful arrangement for the table that day. Flowers make anyone sing and bring a delightful feeling to any table setting. Most grocery stores have fresh flowers, so make it a part of your shopping grocery list. This touch says I'm here, and I love my family!

Other holidays, I try to bring in a table setting to create the mood, including Valentine's Day, Easter, and Fourth of July. Kids love it when they are stimulated at home and using the table as a focal point for discussion of the season, a holiday, or things the family will do to celebrate the times of your lives will add a cheerful dimension of fun. Table settings need not be expensive, in fact I urge you to be frugal in this too. Your local thrift store will have lots of varieties of table linen to choose from and of course, after each seasonal holiday, the table linen go on sale in your local department store.

The other thing I like about setting the table is that you show your family how to come to the table in a way that prepares them for eating out. Your kids should know what a napkin is, they should know where to place the silverware, and the glasses for drinking. It is such a wonderful and lost art to making your table look like you are dining out. I am a stickler for using your napkin, and I insist it be opened and used throughout the meal. Now I don't use cloth napkins for every day, but I do for Sunday dinner and of course special occasions. Napkins are a must for the dinner table in my house.

Parents used to give a daily chore of setting the table and washing the plates. In fact, when I was a girl my siblings and I used to be awakened from our sleep if the dishes were not done when Mom came home from second shift. So, we made the rules including if you did not complete the dishes on your assigned day, you had to take the next day too. I fear that far too many families eat out of a box and, even worse yet, eat on paper plates.

Did I tell you how much we love to wash dishes in my family? After each holiday, it is the gathering place for all the women as we take each plate and lovingly wash it by hand. My mom especially. She comes from a time and place where there were no dishwashers, and everything must be cleaned up before you go to bed, even pots. Here is another opportunity to provide good home training and an efficient system. It makes good sense to grow up in a home where dishes are washed, and the kitchen is cleaned. Tables wiped off, counters wiped down, and sink cleaned. These are the skills you want your kid to know so that they can be successful in things other than a job. Taking care of home and self really count. I also like the smells and sounds of dishes clinking and hot sudsy water flowing over the plates, thinking absently about the day ahead or reflecting on the day passed.

As for setting the table, your everyday plates will do. Make sure you buy a twelve-piece place setting to allow for casual dinners when friends and other family members are invited. I also have fine china. One set inherited and one set I received as a wedding gift. I just recently gave the water goblets I received at my wedding to my daughter as a wedding gift for hers. I had all eight pieces my Aunt Emily gave me, and they were used for every formal dinner we had through the years. The all intact set of champagne flutes, also a wedding set, will be given to my son when he gets married next year. So, there are also advantages to owning your own family heirlooms to remind you of family and all the times shared.

Here is what you need to get your basic every day and special occasion table ready for display:

2-3 table cloths
8-12 cloth napkins
12-piece set of everyday tableware including bowls, small plates (Cups usually not needed, you often have the coffee mugs needed for hot drinks plus they require a lot of storage space)
12-piece fine china
12-piece everyday cutlery set
12-piece fine dining cutlery set
12-piece water glasses, juice glasses, plastic cups

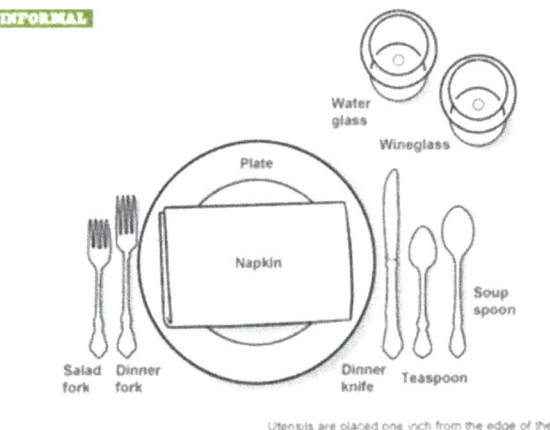

Tableware Needs & Ideas
(cut out magazine pics, staple fabrics & add floral ideas for your table)

Chapter 4

Lunch

Psalm 147:9

He gives to the beast its food, and to the young ravens which cry.

Lunch is another one of those meals that is very important, but you may find yourself losing control for a variety of reasons including the ever-present "time" factor and the fact that your kids will not be with you for this meal. All around the world people stop working and take a break to refresh. Some eat their biggest meals of the day at noon, after having a light breakfast. It is important to mix it up and when providing lunch for school-aged kids, let them be a part of the process. Middle and high school kids need to have a stake in their nutrition, and as part of their grooming and training, allow them to call the shots and make their own. Giving them one day of school lunch is a treat for most. I found this to be very depressing when I realized that the lunch program at the school was filled with hotdogs, pizza, and hamburgers. It is really difficult to keep kids eating healthy when the school lunches were nothing but processed meats and cheese.

I remember school lunch as the time when I took my lunch in a brown paper bag and when my mom used to make these incredible oatmeal cookies that became the source of lunch room trading folklore. That's right, they became epic and perhaps the source of my popularity in fifth grade. The homemade taste of the cookies made everyone stop and notice that "hey, she has something different!" I tried to do similar tricks with my kid's lunch including adding whole wheat pita and baby carrots. Nothing like opening your lunch box and finding something special (like kiwi or watermelon) and mouth-watering. Also, one of my absolute favorites for lunch was a tuna fish sandwich with chopped boiled eggs and relish. To keep the bread firm, just toast it, or pack to assemble.

School lunches have been a controversial topic for many years. As Michelle Obama tried to introduce healthy options for students, many revolted and didn't eat the meals leading to wasted foods. Lunch at school should just be a carryover from what is provided in the home, so helping to create a healthy balance with variety is key. Also, when you have the kids on the weekend, snow days, and summer break, there are plenty of opportunities to provide wholesome options.

For kids, balance is critical as well as making sure that snack foods don't increase their sugar and sodium content. The best options for that are to fill up on fruit, and we love popcorn where you can add just the right amount of salt.

The key for weekend lunches is again to be prepared for bringing the family together at noon for a break of delicious food. Weekends tend to be festive times, so grab-and-go options work best. A pot of spaghetti is wonderful since one pot meals tend to take less time and less clean-up. Also, they can be eaten for dinner by adding a salad or steamed vegetables and rolls.

LUNCH

White Bean Turkey Chili

Ingredients
1 medium onion
1 jalapeno pepper
1 medium green bell pepper
1 lb. 93% lean ground turkey
3 tbsp. Moroccan rub
4 garlic cloves pressed
½ tsp. salt
2 cans 15 oz. cannellini beans drained and rinsed
1 can 14.5 oz. tomato sauce
1 can 14.5 oz. petite diced tomatoes with garlic and onion, unstrained

Directions
Coarsely chop jalapeno, onion, and bell pepper.
Add chopped veggies and pressed garlic, seasonings to turkey.
Mix well.
Microwave covered 5-7 minutes in a microwave clay baker, breaking up into crumbles ½ way through.
Remove from microwave carefully add rinsed beans, tomato sauce, and diced tomatoes, mix well. Cover and microwave 14-17 minutes.

Will you Be Home for Dinner?

Parmesan Chicken Tenders

Ingredients

Package of chicken tender loin
2 eggs
1 cup parmesan cheese
¼ cup fresh parsley
¼ tsp. black pepper
½ tsp. salt

Directions
Prepare two trays for dipping and coating chicken
Wash strips of chicken set aside
Crack eggs and using whisk, stir until you break egg yolk, leave in shallow tray for coating chicken.
Combine and prepare grated cheese, chopped parsley, and salt and pepper pile in shallow tray.
Dip each strip in egg wash, then lay in cheese mixture and press cheese mixture on chicken.
Place chicken on baking sheet (stone is best).
Bake at 450 degrees F for 20 minutes, turning once.

Cool Kale Salad

Ingredients

1 garlic clove
1 bunch kale (6 oz.)
½ medium red pepper cut in thin strips
2 tbsp. low-sodium soy sauce
2 tbsp. rice vinegar
1 tbsp. sesame seeds
½ tbsp. sesame oil

Directions

Use a garlic press to process garlic into large mixing bowl.
Add soy sauce and rice vinegar to garlic, and mix.
Remove stem from the kale, coarsely chop the leaves.
Add kale to dressing, and wring and knead the mixture with hands until kale turns dark green and soft.
Add sesame oil and toss.
Fold in red pepper and sesame seeds.

Chicken & Broccoli Squares with Cheese

Ingredients

1 package 13.8 oz. refrigerated pizza crust
2 tbsp. light mayo
2 tsp. Dijon mustard
½ medium red bell pepper
½ small onion
1 ½ diced cooked chicken breast
1 ½ cups frozen broccoli, thawed
8 oz. Swiss cheese, divided

Directions

Preheat oven to 400 degrees F.
Brush baking sheet with oil (use stone bar pan best).
Unroll pizza crust in pan and press to edges.
Bake on lowest rack 15-18 minutes.
Mix mayo and mustard, set aside.
Chop bell pepper and onion, add to mayo mixture.
Add chicken, broccoli, and ½ cheese to bowl with mayo mix and veggies.
Microwave on high 2-3 minutes.
Remove crust from oven and sprinkle with remaining cheese to melt.
Top crust with the microwaved chicken vegetable and cheese mixture
Spread warm mixture on cooked crust. Allow to rest, cut and enjoy

Easy Fish Tacos

Ingredients
Frozen fish sticks (Gorton's)
Small flour tortilla rounds
4 tbsp oil

Toppings
½ red onion thinly sliced
1 cup shredded cheese
Salsa
Cilantro
1 lime
Napa cabbage thinly shredded

Sour cream
Chipotle dressing

Directions
Prepare the fish as stated on package (Bake 20 minutes at 475 degrees F).
When done, remove and chop into chunks.
Put each topping in an individual bowl.
Using a hot skillet with oil, place tortilla in skillet and brown on each side until slightly brown.
Immediately remove to paper towel.
Take tortilla in hand, add 2-3 chunks of fish, and top as desired.
Squeeze juice of lime wedge
Pinch and eat.

Ambrosia (Fruit) Salad

Ingredients

1 can mandarin oranges
1 can pineapple tidbits (drained)
1 can angel coconut
2 cups miniature marshmallows
1 pint sour cream

Directions

Fold together and let stand in refrigerator overnight.
Garnish with about 14-16 maraschino cherries.

Lunch

My Recipe Ideas

Ingredients

Directions

Will you Be Home for Dinner?

My Recipe Ideas

Ingredients

Directions

My Recipe Ideas

Ingredients

Directions

Will you Be Home for Dinner?

My Recipe Ideas

Ingredients

Directions

Lunch

My Recipe Ideas

Ingredients

Directions

Will you Be Home for Dinner?

NOTES

Chapter 5

The School of Manners

1 Corinthians 10:31

Whether then you eat or drink or whatever you do, do all to the glory of God.

In today's grab-and-go eating culture, manners take a back seat. Not only do we not normally sit down to eat a meal, but when we do, it is often clear that table manners 101 is needed. Why are table manners so important? Well, they were not always important to the American family, in fact, it was just at the advent of the emerging middle class that families began to want to be a part of community clubs and organizations; and therefore, if invited, it was essential to know how to conduct yourself at the table.

I remember a challenging time when my son was on the basketball circuit at a young age, which meant he was eating out all day, every day during the summer at practices and traveling with the team, (a band of adolescent boys and coaches) that may not have encouraged polite eating. So, I had to gently redirect his table manners, which included both hands in the food and eating while talking, in gulps with his mouth open. Helping your kids know how to be socially appropriate while eating will come in handy when they eat out with friends or begin their professional careers. Below are a few tips on how to get the kids up to speed in your personal school of manners. Sitting down and sharing a meal takes time, but it is time well spent with the family teaching kids valuable lessons they will use throughout life. (These may sound old school, OK, yeah, they are.) These are ideas you may want to instill in your children by making them family rules.

Washing hands before eating
A person should never come in off the street and begin eating. It is wise to wash your hands before sitting at the table. There are so many germs on our hands from computers, doors, and all the other surfaces we encounter. It is so important to establish this practice to ensure everyone's safety.

Getting tidied up before dinner
While you are washing your hands, you can also tell the kids to put on a clean shirt or change their school clothes to something comfortable in the house. The same thing goes for the clothes as the hands, they carry lots of germs. Kids who have been working hard at school and on the playground need to tidy up for dinner.

Saying grace
I come from a Christian family, and we always gave thanks before eating. Many religions have this practice, and it is a good opportunity to instill your family's religious and spiritual beliefs by allowing everyone in the family to participate. There was a time when I led the youth at my church, and we taught the kids to pray. This came in handy for prayer time in my home since we taught the kids never to be afraid to pray and most of all, to give thanks. Surprisingly, this ritual gives kids amazing confidence.

Seconds
Obviously, some people may be hungrier than others. It is polite for each person to serve up a portion-controlled plate to begin with. I get so mad when I go places where groups are eating, and one person loads their plate to capacity. This shows greed, lack of patience, and selfishness by not thinking of others who also need to get their plate. The proper behavior is to eat your share, and then ask for seconds when everyone has had a portion.

Eating with your mouth open

The proper way to eat is to chew (Wow, many don't know this). Chewing works best with your mouth closed and with multiple chews for each bite. This aids in digestion and eliminates the possibility of choking on swallowing to much at one time. I choked on some food one time. My bite went down the "wrong throat" I played it off, but I couldn't breathe or cough. I was caught off guard so try to remember this tip: chew, mouth closed, no talking.

Eating more than a bite

One of the biggest potential health risks is to bite off more than you can chew. That is why you have a knife and fork, to cut your food into bite size pieces to chew and swallow before taking another bite. There are many times when teens are hungry and tend to eat fast and gulp. This is a major choking hazard, and it is important to help them slow down, use their utensils, and make bite size pieces to consume.

Picking through your food

Have you ever seen a kid that is so selective that they pick through their food? I was fortunate that my kids ate everything on the plate. That is one incentive to try various foods and for you to be creative in the presentation. It is also an opportunity to get them involved in selecting the food and cooking. I remember my daughter, who is older would often announce what she didn't like and that would influence her younger brother. I had to tell her to keep her opinions to herself and give him a chance to try the new item and decide for himself. Don't underestimate the seniority and influence of the older sibling.

When you are finished ask "May I be excused?"

This old relic of a manner is all but gone. First, we don't eat together anymore, and when we do, everyone is on their phones. Recreate your dinner table as a formal family gathering, and it would be nice if people didn't think their presence was optional. That people understood we need them to be part of the information flow and news of the family. If you need to leave before we are all done, ask to be excused. It says, "I acknowledge this is a place I need to be, but I have another just as important obligation so please allow me to go to that."

When to start eating
It is polite to wait until everyone is seated to begin eating. If you are a guest in someone else's home you wait for them to be seated, offer prayer, or invite you to eat. Show restraint while you wait to be invited through those gestures.

Elbows
Sitting at the table is important, too. You are at the table with others and with your family who you care for; so when you come to the table, you should come sitting up and ready to eat and talk to your family. That means no slouching over the table, resting on elbows while eating, or reaching over everyone to get what you want to eat.

Slurping, burping, and other unsightly sounds
What is obvious to some, at times goes right over the heads of most. It is always unsightly and embarrassing for your kid to exhibit this behavior when you take them out, so it starts at home when you correct slurping of soup, burping after eating, smacking as you eat something tasty, talking while eating (which needs its own category), or eating with your mouth open.

Phones at the table
Nope! Parents, please have a phone-free zone….THE TABLE!. Give each other eye contact, learn how to be present for each other. Even if the phone rings, and you must answer, say we are having dinner, which will leave the person on the other end of the line in shock, because most people don't sit and eat together anymore, and return to your meal. They will suddenly have new respect for you and your family.

Family dining rules you want to establish

Will you Be Home for Dinner?

My Recipe Ideas

Ingredients

Directions

My Recipe Ideas

Ingredients

_____   _____

_____   _____

_____   _____

_____   _____

_____   _____

_____   _____

_____   _____

Directions

_____

_____

_____

_____

_____

_____

_____

_____

_____

_____

Will you Be Home for Dinner?

My Recipe Ideas

Ingredients

Directions

My Recipe Ideas

Ingredients

Directions

Will you Be Home for Dinner?

My Recipe Ideas

Ingredients

Directions

NOTES

Chapter 6

Dinner & Conversation

Genesis 43:25

So, they prepared the present for Joseph's coming at noon for they had heard they were to eat a meal there.

OK, once you have spent all this time and energy planning for meals, preparing for meals, cooking your meals, and getting the family to sit down together…what next? This process will become effortless, and you will not even know that you are doing all of this, and you will be the Domestic Goddess that you say you don't want to be. Next, of course, is that while you are sitting down and enjoying the meal you are engaging with your family. Talking about your lives and what matters in each life. For sure, everyone will take time to appreciate the meal and not always verbally. It can come in the form of moans and grunts signifying this meal is really good. The one I like the best is silence. I could always tell that my food was hitting the spot when suddenly after prayer there was silence, demonstrating that faces were being stuffed.

Rah Rah Cheer them on!
So, what is a good topic to talk about when the family is together? It is always good to include everyone, so if you have younger kids some topics may be too much for them, and you may need to find times for deeper conversations about the news of

Will you Be Home for Dinner?

the day or other worldly topics that could be confusing to kids. Having a multigenerational family is super great because elders at the table make great conversation by telling about their life as kids and little tidbits about us, their kids. Children always get a chuckle when they find out how their parents may have acted when they were their age. So, remember to keep the conversations going, so all can participate.

Another good thing to discuss is your day in review. I really liked to hear from my kids how they liked their lunch or what their classmates thought about a new pair of sneakers. What is important here is to watch for signs of bullying and other kids that may be aggressive towards your child. I liked to ask my kids how they responded to any hurtful comments they may have received during the day, giving them encouragement to respond in specific ways in the future. This I felt was a good way of giving my child permission to defend themselves and to know that they had my support. I would ask about what the teachers were doing when a child tells me of any particularly loud or aggressive moments. Of course, while talking about the day, we would always talk about how they did on exams or other assignments to get their view on how things were going. You should not have to wait for a PTA meeting to find out how your kid interacts with others, some of that should come from the kids. Developing this sort of close bond with your kids through talking about their lives and relationships will yield benefits in so many ways including positive self-view, improved communication skills, and connection as a family unit. If you are not doing this, you are missing an opportunity to stay connected to your kids.

Another good topic for dinner table and family gatherings is "What about tomorrow?" Modern and daily lives today require lots of coordination. Who needs black pants for the winter concert? What dish do I need to bring for choir rehearsal, who has dental appointment and I have to pick them up early? So many things. Oh yeah, who has a game or play practice tomorrow: which often drove daily activities in my family in my family during the teen years. These short discussions on what is coming up tomorrow is something that is always kept on a kitchen calendar, and everyone can add their events to the calendar. Getting the kids involved in what the family priority is for the week can also bring a sense of closeness as everyone pitches in to accomplish the family goals. This is teaching your child responsibility with planning, organization, and promptness. The more you make this routine, the easier your weeks will flow.

Sometimes, and this might be good for when company is over, I like to have discussions about fantasy or big dreams topics, like what do you want to be when you grow up or what is your favorite place you have been on vacation. These what-if discussions always bring a lot of laughter and fun as the kids talk about what they want to see happen in their lives and how they hope to grow through life. Talking about the future and hypothetical situations gets the imagination going and helps kids to think outside the box, and who says dreams can't come true? It always starts with a thought and then as a child feels nurtured and encouraged, they begin to feel that these wishes and dreams can come true. In addition to this sort of forward thinking, the family can do group vision tasks like discussing their vacation and where it will be. Get the kids involved in looking up the information on the internet, and as they get older, they can be involved in planning some of the activities for the weekend or for an upcoming trip.

As discussed earlier, the news of the day is not always suited for dinner conversation with younger kids, but it may be perfectly suitable for high school kids who are expected to form an opinion on what is happening in the world. I'm in no way saying to helicopter your kids because as they become teens you are free to step from the leading role to walking alongside, allowing them to make choices and decisions and even to fail as it is a learning opportunity. So, using this family time is good for talking as a family about some of the things that may be going on in your community or around the world. It is always important to ask your kids what they think about a situation, why do they feel that way, and how they think a solution to a problem may be achieved. You can and should wait to share your perspective and rationale, so if it is different you will not intimidate your kid. If your position is different, urge your kid to continue to think on the matter and to read more as information is available. Remember, others are trying to influence your kids on how to think about different topics, and it is important that they know and understand your values. Often topics will come up where there will be an opportunity to share your family morals and beliefs. We are a modern society that is often accused of not having morals and values, so this may be a time and opportunity to share those values and the reasons that you believe the way you do about broad and concerning topics of the day.

DINNER

Rice & Beans

You can make this to fit the amount you need, a little or a lot. This is super easy and real food. You can add a salad and meat as desired.

Ingredients
1 can black beans
1 medium onion or shallot
1 tbsp. butter
1 cup rice (butter & salt to taste)

Directions
In a small saucepan, melt 1 tbsp. butter. Dice onion and add to butter. Toss and cook until soft.
Add black beans, no need to drain and rinse.
You can also add can of corn or diced red pepper for variation.
You can also try other types of canned beans for variation and flavor.

Make your rice according to directions on the rice and serve beans over rice.
Save time by using a rice cooker. Also, microwave rice cookers.

Roasted Vegetables

Ingredients
(1 cup each)
Carrots
Potatoes (sweet potatoes & small red)
Onions
Broccoli
Cauliflower
½ tsp. red pepper

Seasoning
½ tsp. onion powder
½ tsp. garlic salt
½ tsp. black pepper

Directions
Preheat oven to 450 degrees F.
Mix all seasonings in a small bowl.
Cut all vegetables into bite size pieces.
Toss vegetables in olive oil to coat.
Sprinkle seasoning mix over all vegetables and toss.
Spread all vegetables on baking sheet (stone is best).

Place in oven for 40 minutes, turning mid-way through.

Baked Chicken

Ingredients
1 roasting chicken 3-7 lbs.
Pressed garlic
2 tbsp. olive oil
¼ tsp. season salt
¼ tsp. pepper
½ tbsp. rosemary
½ tsp chipotle seasoning

Directions
Wash chicken, including the cavity.
Using olive oil, rub the chicken all over.
Mix the seasoning and using two fingers pinch and sprinkle all over.
Place in a covered roaster (Clay is best to keep the chicken moist).
Bake for 45 minutes-1 hr., covered
Remove top last 15 minutes to brown chicken.
Place meat thermometer in breast, confirm temperature reaches 165 degrees.
Can use the same technique for chicken parts.
Cooking time may vary.

Meat Loaf

Ingredients
1 lb. ground beef
¼ cup finely chopped onion
¼ cup finely chopped carrots (or chopped kale or spinach)
2 cloves garlic pressed
2 eggs (beaten)
½ tsp Italian seasoning
½ ground pepper
½ cup ketchup

Topping
¼ cup ketchup
Green pepper strips

Directions:
Pre-heat oven to 350 degrees F.
In a large bowl, mix all ingredients.
Shape into a loaf and place in ungreased loaf pan.
Bake 40 minutes.
Remove, and top with ketchup.
Return to oven another 10 minutes.

Indian Chicken & Rice

Ingredients

2 large chicken breasts slightly frozen

1 medium onion

2 cloves of garlic

1 tsp. curry powder

½ tsp. salt

½ tsp. black pepper

½ tsp. garlic powder

½ tsp. onion powder

1 tbsp. butter

2 tbsp. olive oil

Jar Indian marsala sauce

Directions

Cut partially frozen breasts into 1-inch chunks.

Mix with 1 tbsp. olive oil

Cover and mix with seasonings. Let stand (can prepare in advance).

In a large stock pot, melt butter and olive oil.

Slice onion, press garlic, brown. Remove from skillet

Add chicken to oil and brown, turning until done.

Add onions and garlic.

Pour sauce and rinse jar with water.

Simmer 20 minutes.

Ginger-Shrimp Noodles

Ingredients
16 oz. whole wheat spaghetti
12 oz. frozen stir fry vegetables
1 lb. raw peeled deveined shrimp
2 inch piece raw ginger
½ cup sesame ginger dressing

Directions
Cook spaghetti in salted water.
Add 1 package frozen stir fry vegetables 3 minutes before spaghetti done.
Add shrimp 2 minutes before spaghetti done.
Peel and grate ginger.
Drain spaghetti, vegetables, and shrimp.
Toss with sesame ginger dressing and grated ginger.
Top sesame seeds.

Cornbread

Ingredients

1 3/4 cup flour

2/3 cup cornmeal

2/3 cup sugar

¼ cup corn flour

5 tsp. baking powder

½ tsp. salt

1 1/3 cup milk

5 tbsp. unsalted melted butter

1 egg

Directions

First 6 ingredients in bowl

Add milk stirring between each addition

Fold in beaten egg

Add melted butter

Bake 350 degrees F 40 minutes

Will you Be Home for Dinner?

Southwest Chicken Salad

Ingredients

1 ½ pounds boneless, skinless chicken breasts

1 package taco seasoning

¼ cup oil

¼ cup water

¼ cup lemon juice

8 cups torn lettuce

Salsa

Sour cream

Shredded cheddar cheese

Black olives

Directions

In a glass dish or plastic bag, combine taco seasoning with oil water and lemon juice.

Add chicken breasts, turning to coat all sides.

Marinate 30 minutes or longer.

Broil or grill marinated chicken 7-10 minutes each side until done.

Cut chicken into thin slices. Divide lettuce evenly among large salad plates.

Add chicken and garnish with choice of toppings.

Indian-Spiced Eggplant & Cauliflower Stew

Ingredients

2 tbsp. curry powder
1 tsp. onion powder
1 tsp. garlic salt
2 tbsp. olive oil
3 garlic cloves minced
1 tsp. grated fresh ginger
1 large onion sliced
¾ tsp. salt
1 jar Indian simmer sauce sauce

¼ tsp. black pepper
½ tsp. red pepper flakes
1lb eggplant cut into 1-inch cubes
3 cups cauliflower florets
1 15 oz. can diced tomatoes
1 15 oz. can chickpeas
½ cup water

Directions

Place cut eggplant and cauliflower on baking dish. Drizzle with olive oil. Season with salt. Roast 425 degrees F for 45 minutes or until soft and slightly brown. Turn ½ way through cooking. Transfer to large bowl.
Heat olive oil (2 tbsp.) olive oil add onions, garlic, remaining seasonings, and ginger. Heat for 3-4 minutes stirring, reduce heat and simmer.
Add jar of Indian simmer sauce and continue to simmer 3-4 minutes.
Fold in tomatoes, eggplant, and cauliflower. Add water. Continue to simmer.
Add rinsed chickpeas. Simmer. Cover. Reduce heat, stirring occasionally about 20 minutes.

Add sesame seeds to plated stew.

Will you Be Home for Dinner?

Use this work sheet to develop customized family discussion topics.

(Monthly List)

My Recipe Ideas

Ingredients

_____   _____

_____   _____

_____   _____

_____   _____

_____   _____

_____   _____

Directions

_____

_____

_____

_____

_____

_____

_____

_____

Will you Be Home for Dinner?

My Recipe Ideas

Ingredients

Directions

My Recipe Ideas

Ingredients

_____   _____

_____   _____

_____   _____

_____   _____

_____   _____

_____   _____

Directions

_____

_____

_____

_____

_____

_____

_____

_____

Will you Be Home for Dinner?

My Recipe Ideas

Ingredients

Directions

My Recipe Ideas

Ingredients

Directions

Will you Be Home for Dinner?

NOTES

Chapter 7

The Clean Up

Matthew 6:11

Give us this day our daily bread.

It is never too early to assign your kids chores related to the kitchen. After all, this is "Grand Central Station" for every home. A place where you can find shoes, mail, homework, medicines, keys, dishes and food all in the same room! We must all work to keep it organized and safe; after dinner is no exception. It is not solely your job to clean up. Everyone enjoyed the meal, so we all need to pitch in to keep this family brain trust in order.

It starts by having each person scrape their plates of leftovers or if there is more than a mouthful, find a way to store for another meal. Also, someone should do a quick look at the floor and bring out the broom to get up any crumbs, however if you have a dog, no worries he will do his part too. Stacking the plates next to the sink keeps the sink area clear for use during dinner hour and gives the dishwasher a head start with completing this task. The kids should be able to quickly rinse and stack the dishwasher, clean the sink, wipe the counters, and tah dah! Done. Of course, this is not a very hard job because if the cook did it right, she was cleaning while she cooked.

There is also the job of storing leftovers, and that should be done in airtight glass containers with snap shut lids. Once the dishes are done and maybe it is a special night, the small plates can be brought to the table for guess what? Desserts!

The Clean Up

Kitchen Chore List (list initials of responsible party for each day)

	M	T	W	Th	F	S	S	NOTES
Setting table								
Stacking Plates								
Cleaning table								
Sweeping floor								
Washing Dishes								
Putting Food away								

Chapter 8

Desserts!

Ezekiel 16:19

Also My food which I gave you- the pastry of fine flour, oil and honey which I fed you, you would offer before them as sweet incense; and so it was, says the Lord God.

Nothing says I love you like a sweet treat. Keep the family at the table longer by clearing the plates and setting up for the dessert. Some people like to have desert a bit later after eating. That can have some advantages, because you can clean up the first wave of eating. Desserts can be made to be special by sharing this treat after Sunday dinner. I remember that we always had a cake on Sunday. It made the meal special, and as I became a teen I was pulled into making the weekly cake. It was often a box cake, but it certainly helped me to learn my way around the kitchen and measurements and cook times.

I encourage you to get your teens involved in cooking, of course they can help in the kitchen with lots of support tasks like cutting vegetables or getting special tools ready to use. Also, they can be in charge of the dessert. That gives them a unique item to make for the meal that everyone looks forward to. They can hone their skill at doing something that will come in handy in high school when there are lots of bake sales, over nights, and family gatherings where it will pay off to know how to make a simple dessert.

My daughter has long admired the joy of baking and always looked to her Grandma for inspiration with her ever present apple pie. She is now the resident expert of making her own special pear raspberry crumble pie for thanksgiving. There is no better feeling of joy than to watch that pie on a fork then see the responding smile!

Outside of it being a great way to bring the kids into the kitchen, most desserts simply include stirring and adding ingredients, so there is no fear of knives needed to make actual meals. Also, lots of measurements are used in preparing desserts, and that will always be useful in other forms of cooking.

Offering desserts after a meal always makes a sweet ending!

Desserts

Carrot Cake

Ingredients

1 ½ cups vegetable oil
4 eggs
2 cups sugar
2 cups flour
2 tsp. baking soda
1 cup chopped nuts

2 tsp. cinnamon
1 tsp. salt
2 cups carrots, grated
8 oz. can crushed pineapple (drained)
¼ cups raisins

Frosting

12 oz. cream cheese
1/3 cup butter
1 tbsp. milk

½ tsp. vanilla
2 cups powdered sugar

Directions:
Cake
Preheat oven 350 degrees F
Prepare rectangular pan with shorting and flour
Combine and mix vegetable oil, eggs, sugar
Combine dry ingredients flour, baking soda, cinnamon, salt
Add dry to wet ingredients (flour mixture to vegetable oil mixture)
Fold in carrots, nuts, pineapple and raisins
Add mixture to pan evenly
Bake

Icing
Beat Cream cheese, butter and vanilla
Fold in and mix powered sugar adding milk gradually
Frost the cake!

Unbelievable Peanut Butter Cookies

Ingredients

1 large egg

1 cup peanut butter

1 cup sugar

Directions

Preheat oven to 350 degrees F.

Mix ingredients roll into balls.

Put balls on cookie sheet press with fork.

Bake approximately 10-15 minutes.

TIP: Refrigerate dough balls for baking later. Keep in a sealed plastic container.

Sybil's Zucchini Bread

Ingredients

3 cups flour

1 ½ cups sugar

1 tsp. cinnamon

1 tsp. salt

1 tsp. baking powder

¾ tsp. baking soda

2 cups shredded un-peeled zucchini (use large holes)

1 cup chopped nut

1 cup raisins

3 eggs

1 cup vegetable oil

Directions

Stir together flour, sugar, cinnamon, salt, baking powder, baking soda, zucchini, nuts, and raisins.

In separate bowl, beat eggs and oil.

Pour over flour mixture.

Stir until all moistened.

Bake in 5x9 loaf pan in 350 degrees F oven for 1 hour and 30 minutes or until toothpick comes out clean.

Banana-Nut Pound Cake

Ingredients
3 ¼ cups all-purpose flour
½ tsp. baking powder
1 8 oz. package cream cheese, softened
½ cup butter, softened
3 cups granulated sugar
4 eggs
2 medium bananas, mashed (about 1 cup)
¼ cup bourbon or low-fat milk
1 tbsp. vanilla
1 cup chopped pecans, toasted

Directions
Combine flour and baking powder, set aside.
Combine butter and sugar, mix until fully blended. Add eggs one at a time fully mixed. Fold in softened cream cheese, mix.
Add dry ingredients slowly, mixing in between each addition until fully added.
Add bourbon and vanilla.
Fold in bananas and nuts.
Bake at 325 degrees F for 1 hour and 20 minutes

Pound Cake (Million Dollar)

Ingredients

3 cups sugar

1 lb. butter

6 eggs

4 cups flour

¾ cup milk

1 tsp. almond extract

1 tsp. vanilla extract

Directions

Preheat oven 300 degrees F.

Prepare pan with shortening and dust with flour.

Make sure butter and eggs are at room temperature.

Cream sugar and butter.

Add extract.

Gradually add eggs one at a time allowing thorough mixing after each egg.

Gradually add flour, alternate with the addition of milk.

Bake in center of oven 1 hour and 20 minutes. (Depending on the oven you may need to cook longer

Simple Rum Cake

Ingredients
1 box yellow cake mix with pudding
½ cup oil
½ cup rum (can use 1 cup if desired)
1 cup water
½ cup chopped nuts
4 eggs

Directions
Rum Glaze
Using a small sauce pan combine ¼ cup sugar with ¼ cup rum (use more if desired).
1 stick butter.
¼ cup water.
Bring to a brisk boil in sauce pan

Cake
Make cake according to directions
Place nuts in bottom of prepared cake pan.

Bake 325 degrees F for 1 hour.
After cooking, poke holes in cake and pour sugar/rum glaze over cake while cake is still hot.
Let stand 1 hour before cooking.

Desserts!

Easy Brownie Muffins

Ingredients
1 box moist style devil's food cake mix
1 15 oz. can pure pumpkin

Directions
Preheat oven to 400 degrees F.
Prepare muffin pans with liners or spray with nonstick spray.
Combine cake mix and pumpkin. Stir until smooth and uniform.
Pour into prepared muffin pan
Bake 20 minutes or until toothpick comes out clean.

Sweet & Salty Party Mix (snack)

Ingredients:

1 pkg. (3-3.5 oz.) microwave popcorn (5 cups popped)

3 cups miniature pretzel twists

2 cups dry-roasted salted peanuts

2 cups oven-toasted rice cereal squares

1 cup butter (2 sticks)

1 cup packed brown sugar

1/3 cup corn syrup

1 tsp. baking soda

Directions

1) Preheat oven to 300 degrees F. Prepare popcorn according to package directions. In stainless (6-qt) mixing bowl combine popcorn, pretzels, peanuts, and cereal; set aside. Combine butter, brown sugar, and corn syrup in (2-qt) saucepan. Cook and stir with bamboo spoon over medium heat until mixture comes to a boil. Continue to cook without stirring 3 minutes. Remove from heat; carefully stir in baking soda.
2) Pour caramel sauce over popcorn mixture, stir until evenly coated. NOTE: You can use flavored seasonings like chili for a pop. Spoon onto large baking sheet; bake 30 minutes, stirring occasionally. Remove from oven.
3) Transfer popcorn mixture to a large piece of parchment paper. Cool completely, breaking mixture into clusters as it cools.

Desserts!

My Recipe Ideas

Ingredients

Directions

Will you Be Home for Dinner?

My Recipe Ideas

Ingredients

Directions

My Recipe Ideas

Ingredients

Directions

Will you Be Home for Dinner?

My Recipe Ideas

Ingredients

_____   _____

_____   _____

_____   _____

_____   _____

_____   _____

_____   _____

Directions

_____

_____

_____

_____

_____

_____

_____

_____

_____

Desserts!

My Recipe Ideas

Ingredients

Directions

Will you Be Home for Dinner?

NOTES

Post Script

Parents as Advocates—Using Mealtime to get to know and maintain healthy relationships with kids and unite as a family.

Matthew 6:26

Look at the birds of the air, that they do not sow, nor reap nor gather into barns, and yet your heavenly Father feeds them. Are you not worth much more than they?

This is something we instinctively know. That day when we consider our new baby's eyes, we just know, we will always be there for them. We will do anything in the world to make them happy, we will go to the ends of the earth to see a smile on their face. Then life happens, and not so much. Realistically as our children grow, we are more than happy to shift responsibility to them for their lives, but I beg you not so fast.

I know, I know, everyone says don't helicopter, but in our rush to stay behind and let them make decisions, in our zeal to not appear to be a doting parent, in our happiness to see glimmers of adulthood, we sometimes go too far too fast in the "hands-off direction". I like to think of it as our role shifting to one of guidance and support in the teen years vs. hands off. In those years, it is even more important that you establish and continue a strong role of advocacy for your kids.

So, what do I mean by that? An advocate can be thought of as one that speaks on behalf of another to ensure positive results. As our kids are growing up, they do not have much insight into being strategic, and, are not always able to gather information necessary to position themselves for success. It is essential that we continue to lead in providing the appropriate context for the world and the environments that your child is navigating. That requires you to be patient, listen and teach. What better place to do some of that than at the kitchen table!.

This entire book has been about successfully bringing your family to the table not only to nourish but also to get to know, influence & support. Using this time wisely will include enhancing connection and development of relationships with those who work with your children. Here is how to start.

1) Make a list of each teacher, counselor and coach and their phone number and email address.
2) Read all emails that come from the teacher about your kid.
3) Participate in at least two events per year at the school as a volunteer, so teachers will get to know you.
4) Talk to your kids daily about how things are going.

I know that it will not always be easy to find time to talk with your kids, but I continue to maintain that mealtime is the right time for family engagement. If you are not home every day, find time on the weekend or decide to get up early with your child to see them off. Trust that having your family home for dinner will be a fond memory you will cherish for a lifetime.

About the Author

Tany Adams is a devoted mother and Christian woman that strives to share truth to women striving to have healthy families. She learned many lessons while raising her children to be successful adults, and one of the secrets is to nurture them through time and patience. Spend time shaping their minds and thoughts and most importantly their spiritual walk. What better time to spend with your kids than while at the table, the "board room" of the home, the gathering place, and the roundtable of life? The table was always the place where the family rushed to participate, learn, and share.

While the kids are gone and off making their homes and kitchen, Tany enjoys preparing meals for friends and neighbors and sharing her story of positive family vibes with other women.

Tany spent her career in government, is a life coach, and a Pampered Chef Consultant.

Weekly Meal Planning

Day 1 _____	
Day 2 _____	
Day 3 _____	
Day 4 _____	
Day 5 _____	
Day 6 _____	
Day 7 _____	

Will you Be Home for Dinner?

Week of_____

Weekly Shopping List (sections by food types)

Meats
_____   _____
_____   _____
_____   _____

Dairy
_____   _____
_____   _____
_____   _____

Vegetables
_____   _____
_____   _____
_____   _____

Fruit
_____   _____
_____   _____
_____   _____

Pantry
_____   _____
_____   _____
_____   _____

Snacks
_____   _____
_____   _____
_____   _____

Weekly Meal Planning

Day 1 _____	
Day 2 _____	
Day 3 _____	
Day 4 _____	
Day 5 _____	
Day 6 _____	
Day 7 _____	

Will you Be Home for Dinner?

Week of_____

Weekly Shopping List (sections by food types)

Meats
_____   _____
_____   _____
_____   _____

Dairy
_____   _____
_____   _____
_____   _____

Vegetables
_____   _____
_____   _____
_____   _____

Fruit
_____   _____
_____   _____
_____   _____

Pantry
_____   _____
_____   _____
_____   _____

Snacks
_____   _____
_____   _____
_____   _____

Weekly Meal Planning

Day 1 _____	
Day 2 _____	
Day 3 _____	
Day 4 _____	
Day 5 _____	
Day 6 _____	
Day 7 _____	

Will you Be Home for Dinner?

Week of _____

Weekly Shopping List (sections by food types)

Meats

_____   _____
_____   _____
_____   _____

Dairy

_____   _____
_____   _____
_____   _____

Vegetables

_____   _____
_____   _____
_____   _____

Fruit

_____   _____
_____   _____
_____   _____

Pantry

_____   _____
_____   _____
_____   _____

Snacks

_____   _____
_____   _____
_____   _____

About the Author

Weekly Meal Planning

Day 1 _____	
Day 2 _____	
Day 3 _____	
Day 4 _____	
Day 5 _____	
Day 6 _____	
Day 7 _____	

Will you Be Home for Dinner?

Week of _____

Weekly Shopping List (sections by food types)

Meats

_____   _____
_____   _____
_____   _____

Dairy

_____   _____
_____   _____
_____   _____

Vegetables

_____   _____
_____   _____
_____   _____

Fruit

_____   _____
_____   _____
_____   _____

Pantry

_____   _____
_____   _____
_____   _____

Snacks

_____   _____
_____   _____
_____   _____

Lightning Source UK Ltd.
Milton Keynes UK
UKHW050643190520
363475UK00003B/112